SO.ARE.YOU.

A pathway to learning to love, accept, and be yourself through understanding the reflective mirrors in relationships and the world within and around you.

Susie Armstrong

Susie Armstrong
so-are-you.com

First Printing: May 2021

ISBN-13: 978-1-7356427-0-3

Susie Armstrong, MHR, LADC, LPC, C.HT

3829 N Classen Blvd. STE 200
Oklahoma City, OK 73112

(405) 921-9785

Susiearmstrong.com

www.so-are-you.com
www.hypnotruth.com

Do you want Susie Armstrong to be the motivational speaker at your next event? Call (405) 921-9785 or email your request to susiearmstrong88@gmail.com.

Dedications

Mom, you are so strong and amazing. Thank you for your love and support. I never could have done this without you. Seth, my precious boy. Your birth kicked me into another dimension of self-discovery and growth. I love you with all my heart and soul. Aaron, thank you for helping me dig deeper into my truth. I will always be grateful for our connection. Thank you ALL for the dark and beautiful mirrors you have shared with me. I would not be the person I am today without YOU.

PeaceLove&Laughter

Why Read This Book

So.Are.You takes you through a step-by-step process of learning to explore who you are with a series of questions and tools that elicit exploration and wonder. They will help you learn to honor, embrace, and release those things that hold you back from creating the life you desire. The processes and personal stories shared will help you learn to use the reflective mirrors in your world to help you learn to love, accept and BE the authentic YOU.

Table of Contents

Chapter One:

Who Am I?

"Who am I?" Have you ever asked yourself this question? Has anyone ever asked you to describe who you are? Do you know the answer to this? Do you love and accept yourself? Do you know what it means to BE yourself? These are questions I continually ask myself and my clients. Some walk through the door wondering what the answers to these questions could be. I have heard many different responses over the years. One common response is, "I have no idea who I am. I can't accept me if I don't know me." Another answer is, "I don't know what it even means to love myself. I don't know who I am." Some might say, "I can't answer that." The questions seem simple, yet they are complicated for many people. Floating around the world with little to no understanding of yourself can create an illusion of bliss. This perceived blissful state is an illusion and eventually fades away revealing all that lies beneath. Remaining unaware impedes the flow of life. We tend to get stuck in cycles and loops of chaos and discomfort. Does any of this sound familiar?

When someone asked me, for the first time, "Who are you?" I said, "What do you mean? I don't know, I'm Susie." I did not have the awareness or confidence to present a thought-out answer. As I stressed about what to share, I felt hot and uncomfortable. I learned later that I was having a shame attack which was linked to deep seeded insecurity. I was more afraid of giving the wrong answers than knowing the truth about myself.

At that point, I had no framework or understanding of what loving, accepting, or being myself meant or felt like. What I did know, was that I was miserable, and I wanted a better life. I wanted a solution, but I had no idea how to attain health, wellness, and confidence. I was unaware that my environment was providing reflective mirrors with the message that all the answers were inside me. This is where the deep work started for me. Since then, I have been able to share my triumphs, as well as assist others in experiencing their own searches and self-discoveries.

So, how do you answer the question "who am I"? This whole type of questioning was foreign to me until I hit bottom. I knew there was something vital missing and decided at that point that I wanted a better life. I could no longer live in misery. I desired happiness and peace, yet I doubted that it existed. So, I continued to follow the nudge to search for more. It guided me through the darkness and maneuvered me onto a different path, a path of hope. Have you ever thought your internal and external environment could help you learn to love, accept, and be yourself? Well, it can!

I invite you to explore yourself as we move through the chapters of this book. I am going to share with you the processes I have implemented in my life, and describe how they transformed my understanding of myself and others. I am also going to share stories of how clients and peers have utilized these tools to make positive changes in their lives. I will outline several processes of how to explore yourself through some basic questions. I will help you understand how your internal world represents your external world. As the old sayings go, "As above so below." "What's within is without," and vice versa. Our answers are usually right in front of us or right within us. There are mirrors all around waiting to be noticed. These reflections are clues from the Universe that help us unlock secrets to a happier and more fulfilling life.

After years of self-exploration, I have learned that my outer world reflects my inner world. People mirror back what I am feeling, doing, and/or being. Sometimes, these experiences may not be recognizable in the moment and may even reflect what is to come at a later time. I had a profound experience when I lived in Los Angeles in my early 20's. I was working at a restaurant off Pacific Coast Highway called Gladstone's for Fish. One day, in a rush to work, I parked off the highway and quickly got out of my car. I looked down at the beach and saw a man walking toward me. He shouted, "Hey! You can't park there! We can't get out." He was angry, annoyed, and coming closer. Without even thinking, as he eventually stood in front of me, I touched his hand and calmly said, "Don't worry, I'll move." He immediately calmed down and replied, "Okay, thanks." I moved my car and quickly ran in to work.

Later in the day, when I left work and approached my car, I found a note on my windshield from the surfer that I had encountered earlier that day. The note read, "Thank you for your kind touch. It changed my mood and made my day better. I wish you the best." I was surprised, and my heart was warmed. My intention of the incident with the man at the beach was to defuse the situation and get to work. He was an obstacle around which I had to navigate. My conscious intention was not heart-centered, it was self-centered. Yet, it ended well.

That event happened at a point in my life when I felt lost. I had been keeping my painful past buried and I was partying all the time. Yet, years later, when I reflected on this experience, I realized the man had mirrored my inner truth. Underneath all my pain and sorrow was a loving heart.

I was unable to understand the magnitude of this experience until recently. It was profound in so many ways. Even though I was not consciously heart-centered, I received love from a stranger. His seemingly small action provided a sense of hope within me. Every action has a reaction and most of the time we never know how we have affected someone. This man was an integral part of my journey, a moment I will never forget.

When people come to me for guidance, I consider it an honor to walk the path with them. I think of myself as a guide, and my primary job is to hold space as they find their truth. I help them learn to love, accept, and be themselves by exploring the reflective mirrors of their relationships with themselves, with others, and with their environment.

What makes me qualified to guide you and others? First, I am a professionally trained substance abuse and mental health counselor. I am a certified hypnotherapist and EFT (Emotional Freedom Technique) practitioner. I am constantly exploring myself by practicing and experiencing new healing practices with the assistance of other counselors and healers. All the methods, tools, and systems I share with you in this book I have experienced firsthand. I believe I need to fully experience something before I share it with others. My personal journey, as well as the paths of those I have witnessed, will be shared in this book. I have changed identifiable details to honor privacy. I will also reference renowned healers, counselors, and innovative researchers throughout the text.

If you implement just a few strategies described in this book, I promise your life will be transformed.

Your self-awareness will increase and your life will be enriched. If you commit to applying all of the strategies described, then a whole new reality will unfold before you. Maintaining even a small behavioral change for a 6-month period will change your life.

If you are looking to have a happier life and experience more freedom and peace, the steps outlined in this book will help you attain what you are seeking. You will understand the power within you and have the tools necessary to walk through daily challenges and release those things that are holding you back. After you complete this book and continue to apply the tools in your life, a clearer understanding of yourself and your world will emerge. The mirrors all around you will become easier to notice and embrace.

The beauty of the methods presented in the text is that they do not discriminate. That means, that the principles are applicable to anyone willing to explore what is within and around them. I challenge you to take a leap of faith, apply the design for living outlined in this book, and then simply observe what takes place. You will notice that as your perception changes so does your life.

Life is full of opportunities to grow, to experience more love and more acceptance, and to achieve greater, deeper levels of simply "being." All that is required is a desire to change and the willingness to act. Of course, this means you need to commit to self-care and self-love, which, at times, may be difficult to do. But, if you stray from the path, know that there is always a way back.

Make your desire a reality. Do whatever it takes to transform and allow the butterfly within you to emerge. We all have what it takes to shine. *Remember, the power is within you*.

Chapter 1: Questions

1. Start to explore the question, "Who Am I?"
2. Do you love yourself? Write examples that prove you have self-love and then write examples of the opposite.
3. Do you accept yourself? Write examples of how you accept yourself and then write some of how you do not.
4. On a scale of 1-10, what level of willingness are you at to embark on the change process? 10 is completely willing, 1 is not willing at all.

Chapter Two:

Hitting Bottom

"Why is it so hard to change? I've tried everything. What's wrong with me?" Have you ever said these words to yourself or to someone else? These questions are always present at the beginning of the change process. I have heard them repeatedly, throughout my life and my professional career. People tend to repeat the same behavior expecting different results until the pain to change is less than the pain to stay the same. "Hitting bottom" is a common term used to describe this state. Yet, this can be viewed very differently. Even though hitting bottom is typically a painful place to be, it can also be the beginning of something beautiful. At this point, because all the old defenses have broken down, you are now able to embrace new ideas, tools, and solutions.

Defense mechanisms are what inhibit transformation. By design, they are doing exactly what they are intended to do, which is to protect the system. Many are installed during childhood or at times of high stress. Consequently, as you mature and/or your life changes, many of these defense mechanisms are not used appropriately and become obstructions for change. Understanding these mechanisms and knowing where they originate will help you dismantle them. Granted, the defense mechanism's natural tendency is to block your progress. Remember, be gentle with yourself and embrace the process. As your self-awareness increases, it becomes easier to notice the self-defeating behaviors that you have been justifying. It is also helpful to reflect on your actions and behaviors with trusted peers, loved ones, and/or healers. This will give you an important insight and perspective.

It takes a certain amount of pain to be able to entertain a new way of life. As you assess where you are in the change process, it is important to remind yourself that you have specific characteristics that make you who you are. What it takes for you to shift your path may be completely different for someone else

Serena, a client who came in to address her depression, anxiety, and past trauma, struggled with releasing her feelings. She said, "I'm afraid if I let them out, I won't be able to stop." The trauma Serena experienced during her life certainly warranted anger and tears. Yet, she barely cried and showed minimal anger. Her defense programming included, "If I feel deeply, I will lose control. If I cry, I'm weak." For a long time, these belief patterns helped her maintain a sense of normalcy and safety while living in a chaotic home. But after a while, persistence, patience, and love enabled her to embrace new ideas and shift her beliefs.

The challenges Serena faced are typical for most of us. She struggled with letting go of personal blocks because they were assets for many years of her life. She had to walk through fear in order to embrace something new.

A high pain tolerance is another block to transformation. The level of pain you can tolerate depends on your upbringing and the beliefs you have adopted throughout your life. Part of hitting bottom is experiencing defeat. That is why many people resist change. They are attempting to outwit perceived failure because of high levels of shame and guilt. Most of us learn to repress and suppress these feelings because of how uncomfortable it is to sit with them. Embracing all aspects of yourself and of your own behavior is essential when implementing new solutions and when walking through the pain of the past.

We all use coping mechanisms to deal with the challenges of life. Some of these mechanisms learned at a young age will remain helpful forever; others may impede your growth and keep painful memories looping in your subconscious. As you assess your behavior and notice which ones are no longer of service to you, you will begin to understand the need to let them go. Then, shift your focus and remember that even if you are repeating unhelpful behavior patterns you are still resourceful.

New clients are typically either hyper-aware of their struggles and highly emotional, or are numb and in denial. People who are unaware of their discomfort generally sense that something is not flowing. Yet, they are blind to what it may be. After they begin to explore themselves and understand the connection between their thoughts, feelings, and beliefs, they begin to comprehend where they have been. A client named Crystal stated, "I had no idea that I was depressed until I wasn't depressed anymore." She had no frame of reference for her state of being since for most of her life she had felt down. The reactive individuals, however, struggle at the opposite end. They have difficulty regulating their feelings. Julie stated, "I can't stop crying. I don't know what to do. Things are horrible. I can't seem to get a handle on things." Crystal was a master at repressing her feelings, while Julie was unable to contain hers. Initially, both had little understanding of what emotional intelligence was all about. Yet while both wanted change, it seemed that neither strategy had long-term positive effects. Finally, Crystal was able to open and embrace her feelings. Julie, however, continued to loop and did not decide to shift her belief system. It is all about choice - taking responsibility for your life and how you want to live it. *Life does not happen to you. You create it.*

When you walk through life unaware, the world will hijack you, creating fear, lack, and dependency. When fear dominates, it affects our decisions, self-esteem, and emotional and spiritual nature. It turns into other things that block you from the sunlight of your spirit, impeding your ability to love, accept, and be yourself. So, learning to release fear and embrace your gifts is essential in the growth process.

We get used to living and thinking a certain way and we forget to challenge ourselves. I have heard many people say, "Is this all there is?" So, we'd better make the best of it. Life is just hard. Many people hit a plateau and then stop asking questions. Or they get caught in maintaining what is called "family patterns," out of loyalty and guilt. I have heard the statement "that's just what we do," so many times. Have you maintained certain traditions because someone told you this is what you were supposed to do? I have. Think about why you decided to continue the tradition. Does it serve you well in any way?

Questioning things shakes up your mental, emotional, and spiritual bubble. Learning something new can cause discomfort because we are unfamiliar with the process. But simply giving yourself permission to be a novice can help shift your perception. As you move through implementing the tools in this book, it will become easier to embrace the discomfort that arises when your beliefs are challenged. Adopt a curious nature.

14

Instead of thinking, "There's something wrong with me," think, "I wonder what I get to learn as I change." Stimulate your inquisitive nature, ask more questions, and embrace resistance. Change is a beautiful part of life. It does not have to be hard.

"Who am I?" What a thought-provoking question. I could write an entire book based on this question. Many people say, "Why do I even need to ask that question? I know who I am. I'm a wife, a mother, a career woman, a doctor, teacher, IT technician, mechanic, counselor, social worker, etc." These are linear answers. This shows you are not fully aware of your true essence. As you continue to process and explore this question you will go deeper within yourself and truly know who you are.

We are multifaceted beings; meaning, we are layered. Even if you think you are a simple person with linear thinking, you can expand your consciousness. It is about what you desire: the path of expansion or the path of limitation. I guarantee if you continue your self-exploration journey, you will be amazed at the magnificent things that are within and around you.

Throughout my life I have known many people who had no desire to let go of destructive behaviors. They continued to act out unhealthy patterns despite the consequences. When you choose to stay the same, you will continue to experience pain and heartache. Blaming and shaming yourself or others only perpetuate destructive cycles. In this framework there is no room for growth and transformation. ***Blaming becomes a way of life.*** These beliefs feed our negative parts. You have a choice to change; no one can do it for you. You must decide that you have what it takes. I cannot convince you. I can only give you tools to assist you along your path. Your job is to collect these tools and use them.

For many years, I sat in victimhood blaming others for my pain. I looped in agony. I am not proud of this behavior, but it is something I learned to embrace. The person I once was is not the person I am now. But I have compassion for who I used to be, and eventually, with time and patience, I did forgive myself. Remember, as you move through change you may not like who you were before. It is normal to experience shame and guilt when looking at your past. Eventually, though, you will be able to extend love and understanding to those parts of yourself. Recognize that you did the best you could with the tools you had at the time.

Pain is information. It informs you that something needs your attention. As I was told many years ago by a beloved mentor, "The pain will lead you where you need to go." I have never forgotten that. It has held true for each challenge I have faced personally, as well as for those people I have assisted along the path. They learned to embrace the pain, as I did and as you will too.

A few years ago, I was working with a client named Destiny. She was struggling with memories of abuse, addiction to alcohol, and codependent behaviors. Over a 3-year period, she was able to work through a significant amount of trauma and was able to maintain sobriety. Then one day she called me and stated, "I messed up, I'm drunk. I can't make it today." I was surprised because she had been consistent in her behavior and very aware of herself. She was fully committed to the change process.

At our next session she stated, "I don't know what happened. My friends left an open bottle of wine on my counter. I drank the whole thing. I didn't think about it, I just did it. Then I couldn't stop." As she processed the relapse, she uncovered that the core was codependency. She said, "I felt out of control and couldn't express how I felt. I was afraid of hurting my friends' feelings. I couldn't find any relief." After releasing the shame, guilt, and regret of her recent behavior, she was able to embrace the truth that in every seemingly negative situation there is something positive. Destiny had experienced another bottom. The alcohol was not the issue. Deep feelings of unworthiness learned in childhood were the real core. Through her experience, more was revealed and she eventually was able to look more deeply into herself.

Learning to understand what happens inside of you is an essential part of making solid, long-lasting change. It means facing the perceived good and bad head on. Many people avoid change because they are fearful of what they will find. It is true that facing yourself can be difficult and scary, especially when you are uncovering secrets – meaning, those things that you vowed never to tell anyone or even those things you have hidden from yourself.

Secrets need light. The light brings perspective and understanding, which reduces shame and guilt. When things hide under the surface for long enough, they cause dis-ease. The stifled energy needs to be honored, embraced, and released.

Making the decision to change can be simple or it can be complicated. It is up to you on how you proceed. I invite you to decide to change something that is holding you back from experiencing the life you desire. Maybe you already know what that constraint is, or maybe not. As you contemplate this idea, prepare to commit to your decision. Remember, you have everything you need within you. **YOU CAN DO IT!**

Chapter 2: Questions

1. Have you hit bottom?
2. If so, what does that mean to you?
3. Are you blaming anyone for your struggles?
4. If so, who and why?
5. How is blaming others preventing you from hitting bottom?

Chapter Three:

Committing to Change

After hitting bottom, you are now open to new concepts and ideas. This is a beautiful and humbling place to be. It is a window in time where increased awareness and clarity takes place. It provides space for you to experience less resistance and prepares you to commit to change and a new way of life.

At this point, you have experienced enough pain to explore new ideas. The changes you attain depend on how ready and willing you are to achieve your desired state of being. It is about making choices. Some people simply want to stop a specific behavior and once that takes place they are satisfied. Others want to climb the ladder of consciousness to enlightenment. It is all about desire and perspective. There is no perfect path. Therefore, it is important to know who you are and what you desire. The more focused you are, the more able you are to follow through with your original intention.

Some people think letting go of unhealthy behaviors and shifting perspectives takes a long time. Others think this process is easy and quick. Truthfully, the process is relative to each person and their own situation. Pace yourself and be willing to go at varying speeds as you learn what works best for you.

All behavior is purposeful. Whether it is considered positive or negative, there is a reason for it happening. Typically, the core is to get something that you believe you need in order to survive or thrive. There is no time frame for this. Each day, commit yourself to doing your best. Be prepared to let that vary from day to day. Some days, doing the smallest self-love action may be all you have energy for. Remember that is enough.

Autopilot has become a default setting for most of us. We are taught to do things repetitively. This is helpful when you are repeating a desired behavior, but it can be detrimental when engaging in a destructive pattern. Repetition is one way we ingrain behaviors, concepts, and systems. When something is mastered it becomes unconscious, meaning you do it without thinking. Yet, we want to ingrain healthy patterns into the subconscious and delete the undesirable ones. It sounds simple, and it really can be, but a longtime, repeated behavior is usually difficult to change. That is why consistency and persistence are imperative in the transformation process. Learning to embrace change instead of forcing it creates a more peaceful transition into the new behavior. As you commit to health and wellness, remember, there is always beauty somewhere within the pain.

The ego tells us that things need to remain the same. The ego's job is to collect information from the past and relate it to the current situation. This is how we assess patterns. We view the past based on memory then do our best to predict the future. The issue with this is the future has probable realities. ***It is not set definitively.*** If you continually focus on how you think and feel about the future, you will influence the outcome. This certainly sounds like a good thing, and sometimes it is. The problem is that what is running in the background gets in the way of the outcome. For example, if you want to let go of nicotine and the subconscious belief is "I can't do it," then you have a conflict going on, and the negative belief pattern will win. The incongruency makes it difficult to change. When you commit to the process, remember it changes along the way. You will gain more understanding even though it may be difficult to stay on the path. That is why daily commitment is helpful, likely critical for moving forward. You can simply say to yourself, "I can do this today." Then you can decide again tomorrow, recommitting to continuing on your new journey.

Veering off the path is something we all experience, especially with the overwhelming number of distractions there are to choose from, such as alcohol, drugs, gambling, television, internet, social media, etc. Granted, none of these things are inherently bad, but when they are used in excess, they do add to chaos and confusion which impedes the change process. Making a daily decision to be mindful of thoughts, feelings, and actions, provides the foundation for long-lasting change.

We tend to think that we are aware and conscious of our daily choices until we begin to awaken and notice we are distracted. For example, I was on a 30-day cleanse and was not consuming sugar, meat, or dairy. A friend walked up to me at an event and handed me a tootsie roll. I immediately unwrapped it and put it in my mouth. After a few seconds, I realized what I had done and spit it out. I had unconsciously taken this candy and started to eat it. I was not in the moment when it occurred. I quickly realized what had taken place and centered myself. This happens often to all of us. We think we are present and paying attention when we are only partially engaged. As we become more self-aware we begin to minimize unconscious habits.

It is amazing to watch people begin to question their reality and start to change – just as you are doing now. As you continue reading this book you are engaging with the text and allowing what works to flow into your mind, and what does not to flow out. Watch yourself as you contemplate what is before you. Notice what happens to your awareness. Is it increasing? Are you having resistance? Whatever you are experiencing is a natural response aligned with your own values and beliefs. Do your best to allow things to come up as you move through each chapter. Later, we will discuss in depth how to honor, embrace, and release thoughts and feelings.

Commitment is the core to change. It is being willing and ready to do whatever it takes, no matter what happens. Letting go of behaviors and patterns that are initially soothing activates withdrawal symptoms. As you move through things you will likely experience days when you would rather act out in old behaviors. This is completely normal. It does not matter what you have decided to shift or process. It could be issues with alcohol, gambling, drugs, sex, codependent behaviors, obsessiveness, processing past trauma, depression, anxiety, etc. After being in a specific state for any length of time the body and mind are familiar with the related feelings and thought patterns. Consequently, when you face the issues and their distinctive connected patterns, things become uncomfortable and can be disorienting.

One evening, at a support meeting, I was approached by a friend who introduced me to a woman who was new to the group. She was visibly anxious. She said hello, and she was doing her best, but she was distinctly uncomfortable. I said, "It's normal to feel discomfort. You are letting go of something that has been your best friend for a long time." She responded, "Thank you, I never thought about it like that. I thought something was wrong with me because I feel bad." Her thoughts were false and were causing her pain. Many people quit because of a belief such as this. The core lesson here: **Don't believe everything you think**.

It is natural to believe that once you have changed an unhealthy behavior then your life will balance out. In recovery groups, this new state is called the "pink cloud." Not everyone experiences this state, and it tends to end after a brief period of time. Trust me, you will experience exactly what you need in order to heal and transform.

As you move through challenges, it will become clearer how the relationship with yourself, with others, and with your environment, provides opportunities for you to grow. Commitment entails being willing to pause, reflect, and accept what is being presented. Some days will flow easily, and other times will be challenging. This is normal. Increasing your understanding of yourself is a process. As more things are uncovered, secrets begin to disappear, negative beliefs melt away, and more space for love and acceptance emerges. Engage and commit, and remember, **you are worth it!** Now, are ready to leap?

Chapter 3: Questions:

1. How do you define commitment?
2. Have you ever been committed to something?
3. Write about what you felt during that time. If you do not remember when you followed through, then describe what you think it would feel like to be committed to change.
4. How willing and ready are you to transform?
5. Decide what you want to change. Write about it with the intention to gain clarity.

Chapter Four:

Leaping

If you have committed to your process, you are ready to leap. Leaping means taking action; commitment means making a decision. As you continue to take steps toward love and acceptance, there will be times when you are flowing and times when you are not. This is a normal part of the process. Learning to honor, embrace, and release fear will help you move forward. People tend to think they are taking steps backwards when they resist change; that view elicits disappointment. I invite you to think of backwards steps as part of your growth. You are struggling for a reason. Your system is telling you there is an underlying issue that needs to be addressed.

It *IS* possible for you to leap into the next level of consciousness and attain the life you desire. Practicing the tools in this book will expand your awareness and instill the hope needed to attain love, acceptance, and long-lasting change. To help you move forward, we will discuss strategies on how to release your feelings. Each day, commit to doing at least one action that supports your growth process. This is an important beginning for change.

Letting go of old behaviors and practicing new ones tends to bring up fear and discomfort in most people. It is easy to justify destructive behavior patterns because they are familiar, and at some point, they likely were helpful. Brookline, a former client, came in to deal with past trauma and address struggles she was having with romantic relationships. She discovered she was addicted to attention. She said, "I think I'm dating too many men. I don't want to be with all of them, but I'm afraid of being alone." Her heart wanted a committed monogamous relationship, but her behavior was attracting men who were not interested in a long-term commitment. She stated, "I realize I'm not going to get what I want by acting this way, but I'm afraid to let go." The men she dated were mirroring what she did not want to look at within herself. These men were flighty and unwilling to commit. As she explored her frustration, she gained insight and was able to walk through her fears of commitment and of being alone. After embracing the mirrors, the men were reflecting back to her, she let go of fear and embraced being single. She stated, "I like being with myself."

There are many reasons that people are afraid to leap. Some say, "It's too hard. I'm scared. It's easier being miserable. I don't want to feel anything." The key word here is afraid. Fear causes people to fight, flee, or freeze. When this happens, all the blood in the body flows to the limbs, which enables you to protect yourself. All the energy diverts to one system and leaves little energy to access your new tools. Then the fear convinces you to stay the same and the new behavior seems no longer viable. This is how the body and mind convince you not to change. What to do now? The key is not to believe everything that you think and feel as you move through transformation. As you grow, new ways of thinking and being will become second nature.

The mind is designed to the think, so that is exactly what it does. Millions of thoughts flow through your mind every second of every day. We attach to thoughts and feelings, which are what create specific experiences. If I feel sadness, my mind is automatically going to look for a thought that fits the feeling, or vice versa. If you are unaware of yourself, your mind will take you on a rollercoaster ride of thoughts and this will elicit many different feelings. That is why being aware of your thoughts will help you release the urge to act them out. Observing thoughts and feelings helps you self-reflect. Feelings are not right, wrong, bad, or good. **They are information.** They inform you that something needs your attention.

A common belief that runs through human consciousness is that change is hard. The truth is, we make it hard. We resist the natural flow of life and complicate things with negative belief patterns and outside opinions. When this happens, the stage is set for you to distrust yourself, and you then respond accordingly. As you make a daily commitment to leap and embrace the new you, however, remember that change is possible, regardless of the discomfort. Embrace the resistance and remember it is just a habit that is controlling your behavior. Anyone who decides to change can do so. Even if you have tried to shift something in your life and have not accomplished your goal, this does not mean you will not be successful in the future. ***The key is to NEVER, EVER give up! Perseverance wins every time.***

Joseph, a client I saw for many years, struggled with maintaining sobriety from alcohol. He wanted to work through fear and address what was keeping him from remaining sober. He continually attended recovery meetings and worked with mentors, yet he could not stop binge drinking. He then started exploring himself and looking within. As he progressed, he found that meditation and mindfulness were helpful techniques. He continued attending recovery meetings and was able to maintain sobriety for over four years. But then he relapsed and almost died. After returning from detox, he said, "I don't ever want to do that again. I don't think I'll make it back." Soon, after a week of sobriety, he regained composure and was able to reflect on his experience. He stated, "The core is worrying about what other people think. It's about trying to make them happy, not myself." He realized the relapse had nothing to do with wanting to drink. He stated, "I couldn't tell them what I needed. I was too afraid of hurting them. So, I hurt myself." He discovered that a deep fear of rejection had been interfering with his ability to know himself and be happy. His daughter and her son had been living with him and they had been fighting a lot. He said, "It was hard to listen to the two of them fighting. It made me feel bad. I felt responsible, and there was nothing I could do to stop it." He explored this more deeply, and then stated, "They were constantly rejecting each other, which is how I felt. I felt rejected by everyone. Watching them made it worse. I just wanted to check out." He realized they were mirroring what he was feeling inside. He further discussed things and said, "I've been so busy worrying about what other people need that I lost sight of who I am."

The most beautiful thing about this experience for me was witnessing him continually returning, no matter what the circumstances were. He never gave up. He continued to leap no matter what obstacle or challenge he faced. It was amazing watching him hit bottom with different aspects of his life, then recommitting and leaping back every time.

Learning to reflect on what you are thinking and feeling can be difficult at times, yet it is important to understand how you operate so you can move through life with grace and ease. Most of us have not been taught to look within and reflect. This sets the stage for patterns to perpetuate throughout family lineages. Some common unspoken rules are: don't talk, don't trust, and don't feel. They are prevalent within family systems and societies. But, if you take the steering wheel and practice daily being in the driver's seat, you will guide your life instead of your life guiding you. You get to choose which beliefs you want to nurture and which ones you want to release.

The tools I am going to share with you in the next chapters are things that I personally have used, and also have taught others to use as they move through the change process. I continue to implement these tools today as I do my best to flow down the river of life. The phrase "*Life is a journey, not a destination*" has rung true for me over the years. When we focus on the destination, we lose sight of what is happening in the moment. *The everlasting eternal moment, the now, is the most beautiful part of life.* In this moment nothing is wrong, right, good, or bad. *It just is*. This is where you learn to BE. It is the space between the thoughts, the subtle calmness that exists whenever you take a breath.

What I am sharing with you now may seem almost impossible to integrate. I certainly felt this way when I started my own journey. But if I can attain it, so can you. We are all capable of embracing our magnificence. It lies within us. All it takes is the desire to change and the willingness to look within. You have hit bottom, have now become committed, and then leaped. Wonderful! Now, it is time to flow.

Chapter 4: Questions

1. Are you ready to leap? Yes or No
2. What do you think about leaping?
3. Have you done it before?
4. Explore what you are feeling and thinking about as you move forward on your journey.

Chapter Five:

Understanding the Self

Learning about the self is an important part of the transformation process. If you do not understand who you are, it is difficult to comprehend what you need to change. As children, we learn to mimic our parents and our peers. We do what they tell us to do, and most importantly, we do what we watch them do. Our roadmap for comprehending the self begins in the womb. We go through what our mothers are experiencing, and after we are born we watch our caregivers and learn their patterns. As we observe them, we log how they define themselves through their expression of thoughts, feelings, behaviors, and actions. They are our framework for understanding ourselves and our world. Therefore, exploring the past is important when defining the self.

People learn by mimicking their peers. As you mature, you may vow not to behave like your parents or peers. Or you may decide to emulate everything they do. One common statement I have heard is, "I'll never be like my parents." Others have said, "I'm so grateful I don't act like them." On the other end of the spectrum clients have stated, "I had the best parents. They were perfect. I want to be just like them." Each of these perspectives are missing vital information. If you vow not to be like your caregivers, that shows a clear resentment; if you see your parents as saints, then you are not seeing their flaws. We all have flaws. There is no such thing as a perfect parent. But resentments block you from seeing your full self. Therefore, exploring the dynamics of your current and past relationships are critical. This will help you investigate the origin of specific behavior patterns and enable you to understand your true nature.

A client named Christina who worked for several years on improving her self-esteem, processing past trauma and reducing codependent behaviors, struggled with a controlling mother. She allowed her mother to dictate how she lived her life, all the way through adulthood. After defining herself and reclaiming her power, Christina was able to shift the dynamics of the relationship. First, she explored what she was drawn to in the world. She began making her own choices and maintained boundaries with her mother. This helped her separate herself from her mother and determine what she needed to change. In the beginning, Christina stated, "I'm nothing like my mother. I decided a long time ago I would never be like her." As she began looking within, she became aware of how she emulated some of her mother's core beliefs and behavior patterns. She said, "The last thing I want is to be like her, but I see it now." As she absorbed her truth, she embraced the parts of herself she saw in her mother. It was painful yet liberating for her. The resistance to the reflections were keeping her trapped in the past. As she released her feelings of resentment, she was able to forgive herself and her mother, thus allowing space for love and acceptance.

The organic vehicle we live in, our body, has been conditioned to respond and react to certain things based on repetitive behavior patterns derived from beliefs. Beliefs are thoughts that are experienced repeatedly until they are solidified in your system.

Just as Google remembers what you search, so does your mind and body. The repeated thoughts become your beliefs. For the system to keep the belief alive it continually sends information to you that will keep specific thought and feeling patterns flowing. So, changing a belief pattern will change your entire system, meaning that your thoughts, feelings, beliefs, and actions will shift.

A client named Darcy came to me for help with her marriage. She had been married for over 25 years to an abusive man. He had been unfaithful many times, and used fear and anger to control her. When she started counseling, the core negative belief inhibiting her growth was, "I'm not worthy." As she embarked on her pathway to healing, she realized how ingrained the belief was within her. Initially, she stated, "I've never felt good enough, and I've never been worthy." At times she indicated her marriage was fulfilling but it would cycle through periods of manipulation and abuse. She stated, "It wasn't always bad, and that's what makes it so hard. I still love him." She continued to shed layers of anger, sadness, and resentment, and gained more self-esteem. When she realized her strength and owned her own power, she made the decision to leave the marriage. She stated, "I see how not feeling worthy kept me there. At times I still miss him, but I understand how me not loving myself trapped me in it for so long."

Exploring and understanding the self can be a fear-provoking process because of how deeply familiar we become with routines and how dependent we are on them. A common theme I see in my practice is people wanting to stop persistent destructive behaviors. They have reached a point where they believe they are not able to stop on their own. It is difficult for them to change because they are on automatic pilot. They are repeating behaviors consciously and unconsciously and do not understand why they cannot stop. This is one reason it is important to explore who and what you think you are. It is interesting to listen to people who follow certain behaviors because their parents did. Many never question why they do it, they just say, "My parents did it, so I do too." For example, holiday traditions present many behavior patterns that are passed down from generation to generation. Many people believe they cannot alter the tradition. When we get locked into a pattern of behavior, we tend to **NOT** question why it is there in the first place. Some beliefs and traditions are wonderful to maintain and others are not. It depends on the individual and what they deem valuable and necessary. A beautiful byproduct of allowing yourself to expand and flow is you send the message that is it okay for others to do the same. It sets the stage for more acceptance and love to be in your life.

As you continue defining the self, you will begin to understand how you became who you are. At this point, your ability to accept unfavorable behavior patterns becomes more difficult. You are now at a crossroad. You can choose to stay the same or venture down the unknown path of transformation. There are many choice points along the path where you can shift your direction if you desire. Layers of shame, guilt, anger, or sadness may surface as you move in either direction. Your ability to repress dense feelings may stop working, causing you to hit another bottom. That is why making a daily choice to do your best is imperative. At times, they may knock you down and other times you will move easily through them. We all innately know that there is more to life than what our five senses tell us. From what I have learned watching others grow and walking the path of change, there is no actual moment of arrival. Things continue. We are **ALL** students of life and there is always a lesson to learn.

As you define the self, your ability to create space for yourself and maintain appropriate boundaries will improve. When you understand who you are and why you behave, think, and feel the way you do, it becomes easier to distinguish between what is occurring within you and what a peer and/or family member is experiencing. It will be easier to respond instead of react. *You will know where you end and others begin*.

I worked with a client, Jean, for four years mainly about focusing on her relationship with her partner, Elan. They were together for six years and the lack of communication was their biggest obstacle. They were both passive and struggled with expressing what they wanted or needed from each other. As Jean moved through understanding herself and defining what and who she was, she realized how much she loved Elan. Prior to realizing her deep love for her partner, she had wanted to move out and experience independence. She had been financially dependent on Elan for most of their relationship. Jean stated, "I just want to leave. It's so awkward. She sleeps in one room and I sleep on the couch. We have meals together, but we don't talk about much." As Jean grew and gained more independence, she stopped focusing on what she wanted from Elan and began to focus on what she herself needed to change. As she changed her perspective and behavior patterns, her understanding of her partner shifted. One afternoon, while in session, she stated, "I keep having this vision. I see what she wants and what she's trying to get. I just want her to have the house at the lake and to take care of the animals and the garden. I want her to be happy." As Jean shared her desire for her partner, she began to tear up. She embraced her feelings and said, "I want to be with her."

As the session progressed, Jean talked about a duck named Grace that Elan had rescued and that lived in their backyard. Jean said, "Grace doesn't like me. She hisses at me. She loves Elan, but Elan hasn't been giving her much attention lately." As we explored the dynamic with the duck, Jean said, "We both want her attention." Moving forward, Jean decided that she and Grace were mirroring each other. They had a love- hate relationship just like they had with Elan. She was able to see the mirror Grace was sharing with her and used it to move closer to Elan. This improved their connection. At this point, Jean knew herself well and was able to assess what she was feeling and thinking in the moment. It was beautiful to witness her make the connections within herself as she explored her wants, needs, and experiences. The reality within her and around her converged, as she felt a deep love for her partner, herself, and her environment. This paved the way for her to continue down the path of growth and transformation.

The beauty of exploring the self is that anyone can do it. It can be done in many ways with the help of counselors, healers, mentors, friends, family, and peers. Many choose to read, write, or explore themselves in private settings, with little reflection from others. It is what works best for each person. Granted, having a trusted individual around to reflect truth back to you can be very helpful. At times, it is difficult to see the whole self because many behavior patterns that are ingrained are hard to acknowledge. Even if they are not aligned with your path, these patterns have served a purpose. I believe that continually exploring the self will help you expand your awareness. Combining assisted and unassisted self-reflection is the optimum setting for growth.

The people who walk into my office are seeking solutions for a problem they are experiencing. Many believe there is something intrinsically wrong with them because they are seeking guidance from a counselor. I was taught many years ago from one of my trusted mentors that the biggest job of a healer is to help clients realize there is nothing wrong with them. When he said that to me, I struggled to accept it. At that time, I believed I was defective in some way. This one statement sent me on an internal exploration that has assisted me in loving and accepting myself. At that moment, I realized that I too believed that there had to be something wrong with me because I sought out help.

If you believe you are broken, then how can you be fixed? That is a question I had to ask myself. As I have explored this over the years, I have come to realize that I am not broken. He was right! I was acting out in behavior patterns and beliefs that I learned and formulated as a result of experiences I had over my lifetime. I learned new behaviors as a result of knowing myself and exploring feelings, thoughts, and beliefs. There was nothing wrong with me, just like there is nothing wrong with you!

Embracing the self and learning to change how you think and feel about **YOU** will transform your life.

Here's something else to consider. If you maintain the belief that you are broken, find "solutions" from a healer, and do not address the belief, then you will likely give your power to the healer. This becomes a way to stay in a looping cycle of victimization. Granted, in the beginning of the healing process, it is typical that people relinquish their power to the counselor, healer, friend, or peer. We tend to associate the sensation of relief with the one who held space for us during our change.

Exploring the self and learning who you are is a lifelong journey. We are constantly changing. Over time, it becomes easier to remember where the center lies within you. This true center, the essence of the self, is found with your breath. Learning to pay attention to your breath and allowing your breathing to slow down assists in remembering yourself. This essence is the light within you, within your body. Your breath will guide you to that place. All you must do is practice allowing your mind to follow your breath. Notice how the air feels as it moves into your body and out of your body. As you continue to practice this daily, you will notice where it stops. This is your center. This is the space where your inner authority resides. We will explore this in more detail later in the book.

As you begin to understand and define aspects of yourself through self-exploration and reflection, you will realize the power that resides within you. When this happens, an energy will emerge from you. This is amazing to witness. The sparkle that you came into this world with will return. You now have the power to change and to create a new life. This is the pathway to knowing the self.

Chapter 5: Questions

1. Describe what you think "the self" is inside you.
2. What characteristics of your current self are similar to your caregiver's characteristics?
3. Are there any behaviors that are exactly the opposite of what your caregivers do now and/or did when you were a child?
4. Which characteristics and/or beliefs would you like to embrace and which would you like to release?
5. Explore any thoughts or feelings that surfaced while exploring these questions.

Chapter Six:

Thoughts and Beliefs

What is a thought? Most people take thoughts for granted. They do not realize the power that thoughts have. Millions of bits of information are downloaded into our systems every second of the day. These bits of information formulate thoughts which are associated with a specific subject or framework that the person has stored in their mind. It is information they reference when seeking to understand themselves, others, and their environment. On a physiological level, thoughts are made up of chemicals and energy that flow through the body. We are generally aware of our thoughts.

As I assist someone with transformation, a primary focal point is learning about thoughts and how they influence your life. A few common statements I have heard over the years are, "I can't stop the chatter. I can't get this thing to calm down! It's constant." Learning to guide your thoughts is part of the growth process. There are three common ways people deal with thoughts: ignore, resist, or observe them. The goal is to observe them and then let them go.

Some believe ignoring thoughts will stop them. The mind, however, is designed to think. Thoughts are a natural part of being human. So, acting as if they do not exist is not helpful. When we ignore what we are thinking and shut things down, we close ourselves off and are unable to notice what is running in the background. At times, this is viewed as healthy behavior because it mutes thoughts for a brief period. The struggle occurs later when the thoughts surface again.

Patricia, a former client, was a master at ignoring her thoughts. After working with her for several years, she became aware of them enough to make connections with her feelings and beliefs. She stated, "I had no idea I was thinking that. I blocked things out for so long, I became numb. That was normal for me." After processing and exploring past trauma and family patterns, Patricia was able to understand why she automatically ignored her thoughts and feelings. She had learned this skill from her family members. During childhood and early adulthood, it was an asset for her. But as she matured, this became a liability.

Resisting thoughts and ignoring them are similar behaviors. The difference is that it takes more conscious energy to resist them than it does to ignore them. At this level, you are aware of your thoughts and intentionally attempt to shut them out or stop them. This causes distress in the mind and body. Many clients have stated that when attempting to shut off thoughts, "My head hurts. I can't stop thinking. My mind is racing." The sensation of resistance indicates forceful actions are taking place.

Observing thoughts allows you to make informed choices about your behavior. It helps you respond instead of react to your environment. This path leads down the river of life instead of up against it. When you swim upstream, against the current, you inhibit the natural flow and are met with resistance and discomfort. This path is heavy and tiring. Yet, we all tend to resist the natural ebb and flow of the world around us and within us.

Since learning to observe thoughts requires skill and practice, it can be considered an art. The art of observing is similar to mindfulness. You must be in the present when you are observing what is passing by your mind. This is what being mindful is. It is being conscious of what is occurring in the moment. When you practice being in the moment and notice what is occurring inside you, you become a master of observing yourself. *Remember, it is a skill and it takes time and effort to ingrain and refine it.*

Observing your thoughts, feelings, and emotions improves your ability to be mindful of your actions. Whether you decide to implement all the tools shared in this book or just a few, using this skill consistently is guaranteed to shift your life. The beauty of beginning the awakening process is it makes it more difficult to return to the unaware state you were in before.

Thoughts give us information, just as feelings and emotions do. Your breath is a powerful tool to utilize as you increase your understanding of your own thought process. Pausing and noticing how the air goes into your body and out of your body can help increase your comprehension of what you are thinking at any moment. At times, this can be tedious. In the beginning, many people swing from one end to other, meaning they become overly aware of their thoughts. This behavior tends to cause discomfort, but it is a natural tendency of the growth process. We move from one end of the spectrum to the other, and eventually move back into the middle. Exploring contrast will assist you in understanding the self and in shifting thought patterns.

As you become more aware of your thoughts, it becomes easier to notice what beliefs are running in the background. Beliefs are constructs of mind that are derived from thought. They are also taught to us by our family, friends, peers, and society in general. When we believe something, it is not a conscious thought process. The belief has already been downloaded into the system, so it runs in the background. It is the code that tells you how to react or respond to certain things. Basically, a belief is a repeated thought pattern that has been ingrained in the subconscious mind and is now an automatic thought process.

As you move through the change process, you will notice the thought patterns and beliefs that are flowing through your mind. Are they positive or negative? Are you beating yourself up for not completing a task fast enough? Have you been thinking you are incapable of maintaining sobriety from drugs and alcohol? Or unable to stop obsessing about a specific task or person? Are you constantly worried that you will be depressed or anxious? Notice if any of these thought loops or similar ones surface. They are defeating belief patterns that are roadblocks to maintaining health and wellness.

Typically, core beliefs are learned during childhood. Many lie dormant and are activated during adolescence, young adulthood, and later in life. There are many common beliefs that we have ingrained in our lives. Becoming aware of these beliefs and noticing the ones that are supporting your success, as well as exploring those that are impeding it, are imperative actions that enable positive change. As you continue to identify what is helpful and what is not, you can focus on embracing the beliefs that help you maintain wellness and release those that are not. The constructive beliefs surface as you honor, embrace, and release the energy behind the defeating belief patterns.

A client named Todd was working through fear of intimate relationships. He had been in therapy for more than five years and had worked through alcohol addiction, and was now struggling with fear about his current romantic relationship. He had been dating Sara off and on for over a year. They had recently started dating again and both had committed to working through their fears and codependent behaviors. He was exploring his fear during one session, and stated, "I've been afraid that I'm doing the same thing my mother did. I keep thinking my relationship is just like her marriage to my stepfather who raised me." As he explored his fear, he started to realize he had stored a memory incorrectly. He said, "Oh, my gosh! I have been thinking of this all wrong. Me and Sara and our children are nothing like that!" He expressed relief and excitement. Todd said, "How strange, I had totally remembered that wrong." All along, he had been thinking that his current relationship mirrored his mother's relationship with his stepfather, which, since childhood, had not been a happy experience for him. As Todd moved forward, he realized he was looping in a negative belief that said, "I don't deserve happiness."

When a behavior pattern is causing difficulties, the person tends to believe the pain to change is more intense than the pain to stay the same. This belief keeps them cycling in a destructive pattern. Yet at some level, there is still a brief sense of perceived relief which keeps them looping. Destructive behavior patterns and beliefs are not comfortable, but they are familiar. That is why people continue to do them even though they are causing pain.

Christopher started counseling to address conflicts within his marriage and his habit of using food to soothe himself. He was fully aware of how food helped him suppress his feelings. He had been raised with a mother who restricted his intake. He stated, "I never felt satisfied. There was never enough. She never made enough for all of us. I was always hungry." Now, as he explored his struggles with food, he realized how intense his anger was towards his wife. He stated, "I do everything. She never takes care of things. She doesn't follow through. I look at her side of the room and it makes me sick. I've tried everything I know to get her motivated." After discussing his irritation, he said, "I'm too old to leave her. I'll just deal with it." As he continued to move through his feelings of frustration, he realized the connection between the two situations, with his mother and with his wife, actually reflected feelings of not having control and not being heard. He gradually addressed his issues but never completely committed to change. Consequently, he had some relief and was able to comprehend that he was using his wife as an excuse to overeat and using his eating as an excuse to be angry at his wife. He was not able to commit 100% to going within to embrace his pain. He did increase his self-awareness, but he did not entirely commit. This is called trimming the bushes. That is what many people do. They trim the tree and leave the roots. When this occurs, you know what happens next, right? Things grow back. What are you willing to do to make your life what you want it to be? Are you willing to pull things out by the roots, or would you rather trim the tree?

Our minds tend to intensify beliefs. Some are true and some are false. It is your job to explore yourself, your world, and follow your heart. If you decide that you want to trim the trees, then that is your choice and there is nothing wrong with that. But why not go for the roots? You can move through your resistance and fear. Yes, it can be difficult and scary, but it is worth every uncomfortable moment and every tear. One of the most beautiful things about life is that it gives us choices, lots and lots of choices. We can either change or stay the same. Either direction will involve pain. One promises continual pain and suffering; the other involves intermittent pain with beauty and peace throughout. *Are you ready to dig out the roots?*

Chapter 6: Questions

1. Practice noticing your thoughts. Are they loud, soft, annoying, etc.? Be descriptive.
2. What is the primary way you deal with your thoughts? Do you ignore, resist, or observe them?
3. Write down 2 defeating beliefs and 2 fulfilling beliefs.
4. Explore how the defeating beliefs have served you. Write about how they have harmed you.
5. Contemplate letting go of a defeating belief and embracing a fulfilling one

Chapter Seven:

Feelings and Emotions

Another essential part of self-discovery is understanding feelings and emotions. They are an integral part of how we perceive the world, so it is important to explore them in depth. Feelings are sensations in the body that occur during and after experiences and interactions within you and around you. They are how we connect to each other and our environment. Emotions are energy in motion. They are the product of a feeling being acted out. Feelings are contained in the body and emotions are projected outward.

It is difficult to decipher what comes first, a thought or a feeling. Many theories support that the feeling comes first. Others indicate that the thought happens first, then the feeling. From what I have observed in myself and in others, both statements have some truth. Both thoughts and feelings are reactions and responses to our internal and external experiences. Either way, they are connected. For our purposes here, we will use both approaches to understand feelings and emotions.

Labeling feelings is an aspect of learning about oneself. I have worked with many clients who were unable to identify what they were feeling due to a lack of framework and vocabulary. Identifying feelings can be easy or difficult. It depends on what you have been exposed to in your lifetime. Whether you are knowledgeable or unaware of your feelings, this is an opportunity to learn and grow and become more in tune with yourself.

Another aspect of understanding and identifying feelings is that we each use different definitions and contexts in our self-expression. This is based on personal experience, and self-understanding. For example, I was in session with a client named Stephanie and I said, "You seem angry." She said, "I'm not angry, I'm frustrated." From my perspective, her body language and tone of voice sounded angry. From her perspective she was frustrated. So, it is important for you to observe yourself and notice which feelings fit your specific situation or mood at any given time. Remember, if someone views your assessment differently, it does not mean you are wrong. It means you have a different perspective.

There has been a message embedded in our world that says intellect is more valuable and reliable than feelings. The truth is when they are understood together and utilized in conjunction with one another the information received is more complete and provides a clearer picture. As you gain a clearer understanding of your feelings and how they affect you, it will be easier to embrace them and let them flow through you.

At times, it can be difficult to assess all the feelings you are experiencing due to the circumstances of your situation. If you are dealing with your daughter's addiction and helping her get into treatment, you may not be able to assess all the feelings you are experiencing in the moment. This is what occurred for a client named Clara. She was helping her daughter pack her bags to go to treatment for methamphetamine addiction. Her focus was on one thing, getting Brooke to treatment as soon as possible. There is a small window of time when an addict is willing to go to treatment and Clara's only focus was that goal. In our session, after she successfully took her daughter to treatment, she stated, "I couldn't feel much in the moment except some anxiety. I was so focused on getting her there. I couldn't feel anything else. Now, I'm relieved. Yet I'm feeling some sort of letdown of feelings." As she shared what had occurred, she realized she had blocked out other feelings in order to deal with the situation. She needed to be aware and engaged for her daughter. So, she put aside what she needed to process. This is a natural process that takes place in high stress and traumatic situations. Our bodies immediately go into a state where we can handle things in the moment. We are attempting to move out of danger. This is equivalent to the fight, flight, or freeze response that was discussed earlier. At these times, having intense feelings will not help you move through the situation, so they are repressed and suppressed for later processing. There are several terms used for this, which include repressing, stuffing, blocking, ignoring, and compartmentalizing. As you can see in this situation, it was helpful in the moment. Issues arise when you do not take the time to process your feelings and experiences after they have occurred.

Clara knew how to identify and release her feelings and understood it was imperative for her to process the situation as soon as possible. She utilized her self-care tools, which consisted of identifying, noticing, and releasing her feelings, thoughts, and emotions. This freed her of unhealthy attachments and allowed her to maintain a close connection with herself and her daughter.

This is an example of someone who has attained emotional integrity. Clara had been committed to her own personal growth and transformation process for more than five years when this occurred. Prior to this experience, it was more difficult for her to identify her thoughts, feelings, and emotions. She continued to practice using her tools, gaining new ones and moving through difficult situations. She became an expert at knowing herself. She stated, "It's never easy walking through situations like these." That is something important to remember: Walking through pain is never easy. It hurts. Feelings and emotions are messy. Yet once you move to the other side of the reactive feelings the active ones appear. As you continue to embrace yourself and use your tools, it becomes easier to recognize the subtle cues that are letting you know what needs your attention. Then minimal resistance occurs and embracing yourself becomes the norm.

Feelings and emotions are not the same even though, in our society, many people use the terms interchangeably. Think about this question:

"How are you feeling?" Most people have been asked this question many times throughout their life. It is a common question in the healing field. We understand feelings as a typical part of human physiology. Now, think about this question. "How are you emoting today?" Most likely you have never been asked this question because it is the incorrect use of the word. Emotions are energy in motion and are felt in the body.

Let's walk through an exercise so you can understand the difference between a feeling and an emotion. Take a moment and think of a memory where you were angry and experienced hate towards someone. Notice where you feel the anger. If you keep your focus on the anger in your body and release it with your breath, then you are staying with the feeling. If you entertain other thoughts of anger, then you will most likely experience more anger, which leads to hatred. Then other thoughts of revenge may surface. If you continue with this then you may possibly call the person or do something to retaliate. At this point, you are fully engaged with an emotion. You are acting out the feeling. It moves through you and is directed at someone or something and radiates outside of your body. When you are in a feeling you will also radiate that specific frequency, but it is contained and less reactive. When feelings and emotions are not honored, embraced, and released, you will draw other situations at that frequency towards you. ***What you put out into the world is what you get back.***

Therefore, it is imperative to gain understanding about how feelings and emotions affect you and the life you are creating. Most of us want a happy, fun, fulfilled life. Yet most do not realize how much they contribute to the trials and tribulations they are experiencing. Coming to terms with how you influence your life, gives you the power to change it. I refer to this as "owning your power." I continually see people give their power away to family, friends, substances, food, money, sex, obsession, depression, fear, anxiety, past trauma, and so much more. When you give your power away, the typical feelings that surface are apathy, grief, and shame. These feelings have a low frequency and are difficult to move through. Again, in situations like these, it is helpful to understand how thoughts and feelings are connected and how they create internal and external experiences.

Granted, it is important to embrace feelings and emotions, no matter what they are. As you learn to sit with them and allow them to flow through you, they become **information**. They are here to inform you that *YOU* need your attention. None of these feelings and emotions are right, wrong, good, or bad. We tend to discriminate and label them according to our own minds. Some labels are considered appropriate, and others are not, since they limit us on what we can express. Releasing feelings is imperative because if repressed or suppressed you will certainly compensate in another way.

Many people shut out their memories of the past, yet they continue to act out behavior patterns that were learned and acquired during that time. At this point, a pattern of resistance has already developed, which inhibits growth and understanding and creates a fear of feelings. Many people are petrified to feel. I was working with a woman named Jessica who had lived in a volatile home during most of her childhood. Consequently, she was terrified of her anger. Jessica rarely reported feeling angry. When we started to explore her past, she shared with me that her father would throw things and scream at her and her mother. She stated, "He never hit us, but the threat was always there. I was scared of him. I had no idea when he'd go off." As we moved through her past trauma, she realized she had underlying anger. Jessica stated, "I'm afraid I'll be like him. I can't be like him." Her solution was to repress her feelings of anger in order to refrain from being hateful and aggressive. The core belief was, "I'm bad if I'm angry." This belief inhibited her from fully releasing the feelings from her past, but kept her tied to it. Jessica was able to reconcile within herself how she had restricted her healing by believing a lie. She changed her belief by honoring, embracing, and releasing her feelings. After they cleared, she was able to shift her belief pattern from one of restriction to one of freedom. She owned her power and transformed her life.

Continuing to understand your feelings and emotions will help you reach the core of what is inhibiting you from experiencing the life you desire. Remember, feelings and emotions are messy. They happen at inconvenient times and can be overwhelming. Learning to accept them for what they are and embracing them will help your life flow easier. We all experience highs and lows. Realizing that it is normal to feel the way you feel is liberating. Understanding how to release those feelings in a safe, constructive way is even more rewarding. ***Now it is time to honor, embrace, and release your feelings.***

Chapter Seven: Questions

1. Throughout the day, practice identifying what you are feeling and where you feel it in your body.
2. Discuss your definition of primary feelings (sad, angry, frustrated, happy, excited, etc.) with a loved one or friend.
3. Write about a situation where you experienced a feeling and emoted it to someone or to something, or emoted in a particular situation.
4. Write about how you understand that your feelings, emotions, thoughts, and beliefs are connected.

Chapter Eight:

Honor-Embrace-Release

Releasing feelings is an essential step when shifting belief and behavior patterns. Most of us tend to use the intellect to solve things and ignore the feelings that accompany the process. As discussed, beliefs are repetitive thought patterns that become hardwired into the system through constant repetition. When you add heightened feeling at the time of installation, the belief is hardwired faster. This goes back to the behavioral experiment done by Watson and Rayner in the early 1900s with Little Albert. They emotionally conditioned him to be fearful of white rats, rabbits, and some objects. Initially, when little Albert was introduced to the animals and objects, he had no fear. Then the experimenters added a loud noise when he saw them, and little Albert cried. The result was that when any of the white objects or animals were near Little Albert, he experienced intense fear and cried. This is how beliefs are hardwired into the mind and body. When you learn to embrace and release the feelings associated with the belief, it helps you transform the old belief into a new supportive belief.

Remember that *perseverance* is key when it comes to changing belief patterns. Some will shift easily, and others will require more focus and persistence to let them go. Even after following through with consistent behavioral changes, they may surface again. It depends on the depth at which they were installed and what payoff you experience when you act them out. Remember, be compassionate with yourself. It is all a part of the process of learning to love, accept, and be your *authentic self*.

At this point, you have learned how your thoughts are connected to your beliefs, how your beliefs elicit thoughts and feelings, and how your feelings create emotions and draw emotional experiences to you. Becoming clearer on how they are connected helps you see how they work together as the operating system of the mind and body. As you practice using the tools in this book you will become an expert at knowing what drives your behavior patterns and emotional responses. This will make it easier for you to change the things that are no longer working for you. Now we can go into the details of how to release feelings and emotions.

As discussed previously, most of us are taught to repress, suppress, ignore, and/or mask our feelings. I have heard so many different things over the years about feelings. For example, "Feelings make me weak." "I wish I didn't feel anything." "I can't do it. It's going to hurt too much." One of my favorites is, "I'd rather have my leg cut off than deal with a heartache." We have been conditioned to think that feelings other than the ones labeled "positive" are not okay. They also get incorrectly linked to situations. For example, a client named Shannon stated, "If I don't worry about my kids, something bad will happen. When I think they're okay, something bad happens." In Shannon's mind, she anchored worrying with a positive outcome. Over time, her constant worry and anxiety compromised her immune system. After learning to embrace and release her feelings, her perception changed. She was able to have positive thoughts and know her children were safe even if she was not constantly worrying about them. With less anxiety and stress, her physical, emotional, and spiritual health improved.

Most of us are in emotional kindergarten. Even counselors, healers, and coaches struggle with intellectualizing feelings to the point of repression. ***Remember, feelings do not discriminate***. As we discuss how to go through releasing your feelings notice what is going on inside your body. Your body is your gauge. It is your instrument. Some people are more attuned to it than others. So, comparing yourself to someone else is not helpful. Most behavior change takes consistent practice and, at times, will be difficult. Change is typically not easy. And as we age, we tend to lack the motivation to change. But remember, anything is possible! The key is: ***NEVER EVER GIVE UP!***

I use a 3-step process to release feelings. In short, you will honor, embrace, and release the feelings you experience. To honor them means to notice them and pay attention where you experience them in your body. You may decide to assign a specific feeling to them, a sensation, and/or color. Next, embrace the feeling. Embracing means to accept and support. This is the time to notice your breath. Pay attention to how your breath flows into your body and out of your body. Breath is a powerful tool for healing. We can use breath to release the feeling. Releasing means to let go of, surrender, or clear. If you are spiritual or religious, you can surrender it to whatever you believe in. If not, let it go, let it flow out of you. Set the intention to be that what you are releasing will be transformed into something useful for the world. Remember, there is power in intention.

To demonstrate the process, take a moment to think of something that is only moderately distressing. Notice what you are feeling and where it is happening in your body (Step 1: Honor). Now, accept and support it by allowing any judgmental or condemning thoughts or memories to float by your mind. Do not attach to them (Step 2: Embrace). Breathe in through your nose, into the area where the feeling is located, and breathe out through your mouth, letting go of the feeling. Remember the feeling is energy. It has an electrical charge to it. You are cooling off your emotional system by breathing in through your nose and out through your mouth. Repeat this at least 3 to 6 times. Then move into normal breaths, breathing in through your nose and out through your nose. Continue this process until you have experienced reduced emotional and physical sensations in your mind and body. At times the feeling will not be completely clear, which means you need to sit with yourself and experience the feelings longer. If the time is not available in that moment go back to it later. Remember, feelings are information. Be patient and extend compassion to yourself. Some experiences need to be difficult and time consuming. Embrace them as best as you can.

You can also use your imagination to help release feelings. Visualize surrounding the feeling with light as it moves out of your body with your breath. Or imagine a virtual scoop going down into your body, grabbing the feeling, and moving it out of your body as you exhale. You can assign a color to the feeling and intend for it to move out of your body with your breath.

There is not one specific visualization or intention that works best. It is totally relevant to the individual. Get creative! Do what works best for you. If your ability to sense things in your body is a strong characteristic, then notice as the feeling moves out of your body. If visualizing or sensing is not easy for you, then "think it so"; meaning, if you think it is happening, it is. As you practice, you will become more in tune with your body and mind and figure out what specific mode works best for you.

Not everyone experiences releasing in the same way. Some may have clear visuals, others may have intense physical sensations in the body, others may experience little of either. The main purpose is to be intentional and consistent with your actions. Many people attempt to implement change for brief periods of time and are unsuccessful. They think they have failed, when the truth is they have not maintained the behavior long enough to experience change. Being consistent and persistent are primary keys to success.

Chapter 8: Questions

1. Write down how you have dealt with feelings.
2. What are the rules surrounding your feelings that you have lived by?
3. Practice Honor-Embrace-Release daily.
4. Get creative with the process.

Chapter Nine:

Reflective Mirrors in Relationships

What are reflective mirrors in relationships? They are people, places, situations, and entities that show you what needs your attention. These mirrors are here to help you see and know yourself better. They also help release resentment and shift beliefs that are inhibiting you from reaching your full potential. My initial introduction to reflective mirrors was from a mentor telling me, "If you spot it, you got it." I heard this phrase a lot at the beginning of my healing journey. I had no idea how helpful mirrors could be at that point. Later, I discovered **The 7 Essene Mysteries of Self**, also known as **The 7 Mirrors of Relationships**. Many scholars and researchers have written extensively about these mirrors. We are going to explore the first four Essene Mirrors and how you can apply them in your life.

The first is the Mirror of the Present Moment. Here you see in others what is in yourself. The second is the Mirror of Judgment, where you judge others and the world around you. The third mirror is what you have lost, given away, or what has been taken from you. The fourth is the mirror of your most forgotten love, yourself. These mirrors tend to elicit both negative and positive responses. Mirrors are easier to comprehend after you have started to explore yourself and have a good grasp on how your thoughts, feelings, and beliefs affect you.

Mirrors are present in all areas of your life. They are the people walking down the street. They are your loved ones. They are the organizations you love and the ones you hate. Mirrors are here to help you *re-member* who you are and help you attain the happiness and freedom you seek. At the beginning, recognizing and embracing these mirrors can be difficult, as they may resonate with a negative undertone. But as you grow, it becomes easier to embrace the perceived negativity and move into the positive lessons that the mirrors provide.

Mirrors can elicit intense fear, anger, resentment, and pride, as well as happiness, peace, and joy. They are reflections of what needs your love and attention. There are probably many right before you that you have never noticed. As you decide you are ready to face yourself, the mirrors become clear. Of course, you may still nurture your ego and block the mirror by deflecting the truth back onto the mirror itself. Meaning, you may blame and shame others and yourself instead of embracing the truth of what is staring back at you.

It is amazing how many people struggle with looking into the mirror. Facing yourself may be one of your biggest fears. Many clients have said, "I can't look at myself in the mirror." If you struggle looking into your own eyes, then it will be difficult to embrace the reflections others are mirroring back to you. Stephen entered counseling to manage work stress. As he progressed in treatment he said, "I refuse to look in the mirror. I can't stand it. I avoid it at all costs. I haven't done it in years." As he started to understand his behavior patterns, he disclosed intense childhood trauma. Initially, he minimized his experiences. But as the truth was uncovered, he said, "I went to my parents and they didn't believe me." At this point he "reversed the locus of control" into himself at an even deeper level than he had already done. This term (phrase) was coined by Collin Ross (2004), and means he shifted things in his mind to where he thought he deserved the abuse. Since his parents refused to hear his truth, he had to cope. So he made himself be the problem. This allowed him to continue to maintain a bond with his parents and survive his childhood. This pattern was maintained throughout adulthood as well. Looking in the mirror was a shameful and disgusting experience for him. There were many times during treatment where he would ask me, "Do you think I'm disgusting?" I responded with, "No, why would I think that?" He said, "How could you not think that about me?" When he looked into the mirror, he was unable to see himself clearly because he blamed himself for the abuse. In this situation, the reflection was giving him the opportunity to heal and face the person in the mirror, to face his past.

As he moved through his trauma, he was able to understand how he made himself bad in order to live through the abuse. This tactic is strategic and brilliant because it allows a child to survive the situation. Yet, as Stephen grew up, this tactic no longer helped him. It inhibited him from thriving. It caused physical, emotional, and mental stress, which led to many bodily dysfunctions that required consistent medical attention.

When Stephen looked into the mirror, he felt disgust because of his unresolved trauma. He saw his abuser, not himself. But now, this mirror gave him the opportunity to heal. The key for Stephen was to decide to face himself in order to remove the pain from his past. Many times he stated, "I didn't want to come in, but I knew I had to because it's not going away." He realized that suppressing and repressing his thoughts, feelings and memories led to detrimental side effects. So, despite the intense fear and anxiety he showed up and did the work.

As he moved through treatment, he was able to recognize that he did not make the abuse happen. This enabled him to embrace the scared little boy in the mirror. Learning to love the scared little boy inside him allowed him to embrace his truth and forgive himself and his abuser. This paved the path for him to embrace other mirrors that were prevalent in his world. His intense need to blame and shame reduced drastically as he courageously looked at himself and the world around him.

The Mirror of Judgment is lacking compassion for what you see in others and yourself. Basically, the thought pattern is that I am better than or I am less than other people. For example, a client named Eva was struggling with a co-worker named John and how he was treating her and others. She came in for a session and was angry and frustrated. She stated, "Who does he think he is? I don't understand how he can justify treating us that way? We're all sick of it." During this time there was added stress in their department due to unforeseen work circumstances. After Eva assessed the situation, she realized she was judging John's behavior. She said, "I don't see how I'm acting like him. I treat him well. I'm not behaving that way at home or with friends." She then explored further and stated, "I have behaved that way before, but I'm not doing it now. And he should know better." As we explored more, we discussed how she was experiencing judgment and condemnation. She felt "better than" and was "looking down upon" John. As Eva experienced the second mirror, she was able to honor, embrace, and release her feelings. John became her teacher instead of her adversary. Eva let go of her resentment and was able to flow through her workday with ease. She stated, "At times, he still irritates me, but now I take a breath and let it go and move on. It's so freeing."

The third mirror is the Mirror of Loss. This mirror is perceiving that you have lost something or someone. Have you ever admired anyone? Or wanted to have what they have? Or felt that someone took something from you? Or regretted giving something away? I am confident in saying most of the people on this planet would say yes to all of these. This represents the Mirror of Loss. Here, you believe you have lost something and need it back. You yearn for that thing or that part of you that you believe was taken from you, or that you lost or gave away. These attachments cause suffering and a deep sense of loss that lingers. So this mirror is here to help you realize that you have everything within you. Once you recognize the beauty in this mirror you can release your attachments and regain all the things you believed were lost. When you let go, they reappear.

Diane, a long-term client, utilized this mirror as she walked through a difficult relationship. Diane had been sober for many years from drugs and alcohol. She experienced a traumatic childhood and struggled with romantic relationships. During her treatment, she dated a man named Brian for whom she had an intense attraction. She stated, "I met him at a workshop, and he was so funny and free.

Afterwards, we connected on social media and I remember looking at his profile. I felt scared that he wouldn't think I was good enough for him. He had so many accomplishments." As she moved through the relationship, she realized that she wanted what he had and believed she did not have any of it within herself. At one point she said, "I'm afraid to be myself. I'm afraid he won't like me because he has it all together and I don't." As the relationship continued, Diane gained clarity and saw inconsistencies in his behavior. "I think he's lying about a lot of things. My guts are constantly churning. It's hard because I believe him when I'm with him. But as soon as he's gone, there's something that eats at me." She stated, "I want to leave him all the time, but can't. Something keeps me holding on." As she explored her connection with him, she said, "He's so funny and exciting but then he's distant and nonresponsive. It's confusing and it hurts."

Diane was continually looking at her behavior and shifting her thoughts, beliefs, and perceptions throughout the relationship. She was able to recognize the first two mirrors with ease and used them to shift her thoughts and release her feelings. When she recognized the third mirror fully within this relationship, it had a profound effect on her. She said, "I have everything he does! He's not better than me. I put him on a pedestal. Not anymore!" She recognized what the third mirror was teaching her, which was that she actually had everything within her that she wanted from Brian. This awareness helped her behave differently in the relationship. She started to stand up for herself and have tough conversations with Brian. Then things shifted again for her.

During the Holiday season Brian unexpectedly ended the relationship. She stated, "He broke up with me through text. He said, "I'm overwhelmed with work, I can't keep my life together. I'm not getting enough sleep. I need to get healthy so that I can have a healthy relationship." Diane stated, "I was devastated. But I understood what he needed. At first, I tried to convince him to stay with me. Then I felt a deep love for him and I let him go. At that moment something happened. I realized I loved myself! It was so profound and amazing!" During the relationship, Diane had been seeking what she thought she had lost, which was her long-lost love, herself. As she sobbed, the truth moved from her head to her heart. At that moment, she experienced pure love for herself.

Even though this relationship was difficult for Diane and Brian, it was a lesson in forgiveness, honesty, and love. When we view relationships in a linear fashion, we miss the gifts that are right before us. Sometimes relationships are supposed to be difficult. When we are challenged by someone we love, it gives us the opportunity to explore the thoughts, feelings, and beliefs that surface during these times. Without challenges, we tend to stagnate and become complacent. I invite you to review your past relationships and explore where you may have forgotten your long-lost love, yourself.

Remember, as you practice noticing reflective mirrors, give yourself time and space to understand them. Over time they become clearer and easier to notice. Each day, set the intention to be open to them and watch what happens. Talk about them with a trusted friend, loved one, or healer. Honor, embrace, and release any feelings that arise when you notice them. Extend compassion to yourself, and remember that mirrors are here for your highest good. Mirrors are here to help you love, accept, and BE yourself.

Chapter 9: Questions

1. Write about where you have experienced each of the four mirrors in your relationships. Mirror 1-the present moment. If you spot it, you got it. Remember the positive ones too!

2. Mirror 2-judgement. How are you judging others?

3. Mirror 3-loss. What you gave away, lost, or what was taken from you.

4. Mirror 4-reflection of your long-lost love, yourself.

5. Practice recognizing these mirrors in your life and how they can help you honor, embrace, and release feelings.

Chapter Ten:

Embracing Mirrors with Forgiveness and Love

As you expand your understanding of reflective mirrors in relationships, you can begin to experience deeper forgiveness and love for yourself and others. Many platforms, counselors, healers, religious and spiritual organizations talk about forgiveness and its association with peace and love. So, as we move through this chapter, we are going to explore the meaning of forgiveness and ways to attain it within yourself. We are also going to discuss love and its many forms. Since not every method works for each person I will provide several examples of how people have embraced reflective mirrors in their lives.

Forgiveness is something that many struggle with. It can be an abstract concept. The Merriam Webster dictionary simply states, "Forgiveness is the act of forgiving." As you can see, that is not much of an explanation for what forgiveness is and how to attain it. I have been asked many times, "How can I forgive them for what they did to me? They were wrong." Forgiveness can be especially difficult for people who have experienced abuse and neglect. They tend to believe that if they forgive their abuser then they condone the behavior. Cecilia had experienced physical abuse from a former boyfriend, and she saw him one night when she was out with some friends. During her session she stated, "I wasn't angry at him. I felt numb and I didn't look at him or acknowledge that he was there." As she explored her thoughts and feelings she stated, "It's strange because I feel I'm saying it's okay that he beat me if I completely forgive him." I said, "Do you think you have to interact with him if you forgive him?" She thought for a moment and said, "Yes, I think so. If I forgive him, I'm saying it never happened." As we move through the session Cecilia was able to embrace her fear of letting go of her victim stance. That mindset had been a way of life for her and had provided her with a sense of safety for many years. Her beliefs surrounding her experience caused resistance in attaining forgiveness which made letting it go a process.

Forgiveness is about letting go of resentments and anger. These feelings are present within the individual and can only be resolved within that person. Many people seek forgiveness, meaning they want someone to apologize for hurting them. I did this for years with my mother. I continually gave her amends for my behavior, subconsciously hoping she would give me one for how she treated me while I was growing up. It never worked. Consequently, I experienced more anger. After a lot of pain, I realized what I was doing, and I stopped seeking forgiveness outside of myself. I wanted her to change so I would be okay. I was struggling with accepting the mirrors I saw in her that were in me. I was demanding, critical, and condescending. I also blamed her for messing up my life. After humbling myself and embracing the shame I felt and then releasing it, I realized she did the best she could do with the tools she had at the time. At that point, I was able to forgive her.

After that, amazing things started to happen. Her behavior toward me changed. She started to be more emotionally present and supportive. One main event I remember was when I was ill and had to go to the hospital. I had been struggling with some physical symptoms that were concerning and anxiety provoking. So, I went to the hospital. I was hesitant to call my mom because she would get angry at me when I was sick. This was associated with caring for her chronically ill mother. I went ahead and called her. She said, "I'll be right there. Everything's going to be okay." When she arrived at the emergency room, she was calm and loving. She held my hand and listened. I felt love and support from her that I had never experienced. It was beautiful.

We discussed the situation at length at another time and she said, "I wanted to be different for you. I knew there was nothing I could say to change what I had done in the past, so I showed up for you. I didn't get mad. I love you. I'm sorry for not being there for you before." Another amazing moment of forgiveness. If I would have continued to seek forgiveness outside of myself, the space would never have been created for us to experience this together. By freeing myself, I helped free her, which finally freed us.

It can be difficult to embrace the mirrors you see in your world. They are humbling. Our egos are fragile, and they resist admitting things that invoke guilt or shame. That is why most people tend to get angry at someone or something before they realize it is a reflective mirror that is giving them an opportunity to let go and heal.

Samantha was seeking counseling to help her exit a difficult marriage. As she started to explore her behavior patterns, she gained insight and was able to understand how she put herself in her current situation because of negative beliefs she learned while growing up. Initially, the main concern was leaving the relationship. She stated, "I can't take it anymore. I feel trapped." They were waiting to separate because of financial reasons. Consequently, there was a period where they were living together even though they were separated. Eventually, they filed for divorce. As Samantha worked through her anger and grief she would continually say, "He'll never do the work he needs to. He's always procrastinating. He never follows through. It's been hopeless from the beginning."

After exploring her own behavior through the divorce, she had a pivotal moment where she saw the reflection clearly. She said, "Oh my gosh! I see it now. I've been doing the same thing. I procrastinate with my writing all the time and have for 30 years!" At this point her face softened and she shed some tears. She saw how her anger was primarily at herself not at her husband. At this point, moving through the divorce was easier. She embraced the mirrors with forgiveness, allowing her to engage in her own life more easily.

Initially, Samantha was unable to understand that her behavior was the same as her husband's. She resisted looking at the similarities. This is what most people struggle with because of the shame associated with realizing your behavior is like the person's whom you resent. When you are engaged in anger or resentment, it is difficult to access empathy. This makes letting go a struggle. The shame lurking underneath needs to be addressed. Since anger is a higher vibrating feeling, it becomes another obstacle in being able to experience the gifts of reflective mirrors in relationships. When you can experience the pain underneath the anger, it allows space for empathy. As the mind calms down, reality softens and gets clear, just as Samantha's face did when she realized she was angry at herself. This softness allowed her to embrace the reflective mirrors in her marriage with forgiveness and love.

The power in taking responsibility for you own thoughts and feelings is tremendous. It will set you free and provide the space for peace. You can control what happens inside you. Even though at times it seems you are unable to do that, you truly can. But controlling someone else is not possible. You can manipulate or be manipulated into doing things you do not want to do. The truth is, at some level, there is awareness that you are giving your power away or that someone is giving it to you. Understanding yourself and bringing the darkness within you to light, is imperative for true forgiveness, love, and ultimate freedom.

Chapter 10: Questions

1. What does forgiveness mean to you?
2. Explore and write about a time when you have noticed a reflective mirror in your relationship that brought up shame or guilt.
3. How did you handle the feelings that surfaced during this situation discussed in question #2?
4. Were you able to resolve things within yourself and embrace forgiveness and love? If not, attempt to start the process now.

Chapter Eleven:

Acceptance to Freedom

As you continue to notice the reflective mirrors in your environment your ability to accept them as gifts of truth becomes easier. They are not here to harm you even when they bring up uncomfortable memories, thoughts, and feelings. Yet, at times the pain is too much to bear, so the mirror remains unseen. The beauty is that another will arrive at the perfect time giving you the opportunity to heal the wound that was buried deep within you. Remember, as you continue to accept what and who you are, embracing your reflections becomes part of life. You naturally notice them. Since I have been embracing them for some time now, I notice them daily. They are a part of my reality and help remind me of my center. Granted, at times I experience resistance to what I am being shown. This is where I implement honoring, embracing, and releasing the feelings and thoughts associated with the mirror. Now, there is room for acceptance, creating the space to see the mirror clearly.

Have you experienced acceptance and freedom after noticing a reflective mirror in your life? If not, have you experienced a sense of release when you have let go of resentment or anger towards someone? If so, this is a similar experience. Exploring mirrors enriches the experience and provides another view to explore. If you have not experienced either, do not be discouraged. You will have relief. It is possible that you have experienced it without knowing it. Awareness is key. Since our lives move quickly it is easy to remain unaware of many things. Making the decision to explore who and what you are is a wise choice. As you continue to self-reflect and become more comfortable within yourself, loving yourself becomes a natural state of being. Love is freedom from the attachments of the negative belief patterns that inhibit us from experiencing true freedom.

When faced with a difficult mirror that brings up intense shame and guilt, many maintain a stance of blame and anger, especially when the judgement mirror is showing itself. Selina was struggling with a difficult marriage because of infidelity. Through a family friend, she found out that her husband was cheating on her. She stated, "I'm still in shock. I never thought that would happen. I didn't see it coming." As she moved through her thoughts and feelings, she decided to stay with him and attempt to work things out. Months later, they seemed to have healed somewhat and were reconnecting. He started counseling and was remorseful. During a session Selina stated, "I realized I've been punishing him. I haven't let him back in completely. I've been pretending. I'm still resentful of what he did to me." As she admitted the motive behind her behavior, she was able to understand that she had been judging him for what he had done. As she embraced her judgement, she was able to accept her part during the marriage where she was closed off and avoidant. She stated, "I had so many signs that he was unhappy and cheating, and I chose to ignore them. I wasn't going to go through that again. So I closed myself off." As Selina honored, embraced, and released her judgment she experienced acceptance and love. She stated, "This has been so hard, but I wouldn't have it any other way. I've learned so much."

Since Selina continued to explore her thoughts, feelings, and beliefs she eventually reached a point of acceptance. The growth I witnessed within her was one of the most beautiful things I have ever experienced. Selina continued embracing herself and living in her truth. She eventually left her husband, but with his true support. They healed. In spite of the betrayal they grew together. This is a lesson in acceptance and freedom to the fullest.

As I walked with Selina through this part of her life, I had no idea where it was going. As things unfolded, I sat back and supported her where she needed me. I, too, had to embrace the mirror of judgement through this process and let it go. When they showed themselves, I honored, embraced, and released my feelings, letting go of any attachments that could affect the outcome and my ability to hold space for Selina. This practice allowed me to be present for her. Maintaining neutrality is not easy. We are designed to attach to thoughts, feelings, and beliefs. That is why ongoing self-reflection helps ingrain tools that assist you in staying in the moment.

Throughout my life and career, I have been told to let it go, accept it and it will all be okay. Granted, I agree with these concepts; however this is easier said than done. Acceptance of oneself and one's world allows for freedom to flow. Yet, along the way there are always bumps in the road and letting go may not be something that feels doable. Have you ever wallowed in anger? Or maybe sadness or fear? I know I have. The difficult part is when these feelings linger and there seems to be no solution in sight. I have experienced this, off and on, during my life, even after noticing the mirrors and implementing the tools outlined in this book. What I realized was that I was not fully embracing the situation. I honored it, slightly embraced it, and then promptly moved to releasing it. Consequently, there was residue left that needed attention. So, if you find yourself looping in feelings and thoughts, create more space to embrace them.

I have witnessed many clients doing the same thing. We are creatures of habit and tend to avoid pain at all cost, especially emotional pain. So, quickly moving through embracing it is a natural tendency for most people. Reality is, though, that embracing takes time and effort. It is about being gentle with yourself and learning to sit with your wounded parts. Sitting in shame is one of the most uncomfortable things to learn to do. Yet the beauty is that after doing it once, you can do it again and again. Remember, you are increasing self-awareness and practicing healthy habits. This takes consistency and persistence.

What does freedom mean to you? Contemplate that for a moment. It is a complex question. Are you free? Defining freedom is an important step as you move through the transformation process. Many people associate the word freedom with not being restricted or enslaved, and being allowed to express oneself in an appropriate, personal manner. Here we are discussing personal and internal freedom. Do you feel trapped in your body, in your life, or in the way you think? Those are the questions to ponder as you explore freedom. There have been many accounts of people who have been in prison for most of their lives, who actually found freedom from the mind while being stripped of physical freedom. It is the confines of our minds that entrap us in belief and behavioral patterns that cause suffering.

Experiencing freedom within is a byproduct of grasping reflective mirrors in relationships. As you continue to notice the mirrors all around you and realize your connection with all things, the walls begin to come down around you. It becomes easier to release resentment and anger, and you can now make room for peace, love, and joy. We are all at different levels of understanding in the game of life. So, doing your part is giving to the whole. When you see something beautiful as you are driving down the street, walking in a park, or shopping at a store, remember the beauty you are seeing is also within you. At this point, notice the sensations in your body. What do you feel? Are there flutters of energy or sensations in your chest, your hands, your legs, your whole body? Just notice. That is freedom from the bondage of self. The bondage of the old ways the old ideas of who you thought you were. You are now a new person. You may move back to the old ways when fear, sadness, or anger arises, but you can always move back into the new you, the one who sees, knows, and understands the truth that you have the power within you to be whatever you want to be.

Chapter 11: Questions

1. Define acceptance.
2. What is freedom? Define all levels – emotional, physical, spiritual.

3. Write about an experience where you have used a mirror to move into acceptance.

4. Write down 5 loving statements about yourself. Read them daily.

Chapter Twelve:

Implementation

In this chapter, we are going to discuss implementing the tools, concepts, and exercises discussed throughout this book. Many of you may have already started exploring who you are, practicing honoring, embracing, and releasing your feelings and observing the reflective mirrors in your life. Some of you are waiting to complete the book before implementing the tools discussed. Whichever way you decide to move forward is up to you. At this point, new ideas and concepts about yourself are emerging. This book is designed to shake your personal bubble, shifting your perception of yourself to something wonderful, fresh, and honest. Even though you may initially be uncomfortable, remember that the journey is also exciting. You are on a new voyage of self-exploration and wonder that is intended to help you love, accept, and be the authentic you.

Has your perception of yourself shifted since you started reading this book? If not, it will. Remember, you are changing, so your view of yourself will continually shift as you move down the path. Periodically, reflect on the question, "Who am I?" and notice what surfaces. Pay attention to the thoughts, feelings, and beliefs that surround what you think of yourself and how you define who you are. This will help you decide what you would like to maintain and what you would like to change about yourself.

After making your decision, then assess if you have hit bottom. Ask yourself if you are ready to stop doing what is causing you unnecessary pain and discomfort. Whether you fully shift after implementation of some tools in this book or you only slightly shift, you have increased your self-awareness. This is the key.

Focus on one behavior you know is causing disruption in your life. Journal about how it has served you in a positive way, then explore how it has become harmful. This will help you hit bottom if you have not yet done so. Remember, all behavior is purposeful. At one point, there likely was a positive reason to maintain the behavior. For example, if you struggle with social anxiety then drinking alcohol may provide a temporary reprieve from the anxiety but it will not address the core issue. Afterwards, continued use of alcohol becomes the problem. Drinking was intended to be a helpful action, not a harmful one, in the beginning. Later it became a disruption. This is true for all behavior. Initially, there is a perceived positive payoff. Once you identify what that is, it is easier to replace the destructive behavior with a supportive one.

Are you ready to commit to change and let go of what is no longer serving you? Remember, it is normal to fear change. We are creatures of habit and we maintain the familiar in order to reduce, repress, and/or avoid pain. Commitment means you will do anything it takes to attain a goal or reach a desired state. Sometimes you may think you want to give up, but that does not mean you will. There are always steps backwards in the change process. This means you may have missed something that needs your attention. It does not mean you have failed. It may feel like failure, but it is not. It is another opportunity to embrace yourself and learn something new and exciting about you and the world around you.

Set a broad and inclusive intention. A good example of this is, I am committed to being the best person I can be. Use this one or another that fits better for you. Stay true to your intention, daily. Write it down and post it around your house or work area. The brain is 50% visual, so noticing intentions and affirmations around your environment will *re-mind* you of the truth that you are a masterful creator of your world. These are actions associated with leaping. You are actively moving along the path of transformation. The life you have been living is still the dominant program running in your system, so constant reminders are helpful as you solidify the new you and the new world around you.

You are now fully committed and leaping. The change process has begun and your awareness has increased. At this point, it is difficult and almost impossible to return to your previous state. You can continue to act out in defeating patterns, but you are now awake. This makes it difficult to numb out the world within and around you. This is a wonderful place to be. Yes, at times it is uncomfortable, but it means you are ready and willing to move through the blocks that keep you from loving, accepting, and being yourself.

As you move through exploring who you are and embracing what it is you want to change notice the thoughts that are dominating your mind. Are they positive or negative? What are the common themes? This will help you identify what belief patterns are associated with any resistance you may be experiencing. ***Remember, a belief is a thought that has been repeated and was hardwired with feelings and emotions.***

At times, identifying the restrictive belief patterns can be simple, and at other times frustrating. If you are struggling with making connections, sit with your frustration. Honor that you are having the feeling. Embrace it with a supportive thought such as, I know you are there. If, you notice where you sense the feeling in your body place your hand on that area. This is also a supportive action. Then take a deep breath into that area with the intention to release the feeling. You are now honoring, embracing, and releasing the frustration. As you continue to practice this, notice what thoughts cross your mind. Do your best not to attach to them. Allow them to float by like puffy clouds in the sky.

If you notice you are following them on a thought trail of destructive thinking simply put your focus back on your breath. ***Your breath is life***.

As you continue to travel on the path of transformation, practice embracing thoughts, feelings, and beliefs. Explore who you are and what you want to become. The reflective mirrors in your relationship are present all around you. Have you started to notice them? Are they clear or muddy? Your job is to ***wonder*** what they are here to teach you. ***Wonder is the key***. If you find yourself searching for what is wrong with you then you have veered off the path. Not to worry, all you must do is shift your focus back to wonder. There is nothing wrong with you and there never has been. This is one of the biggest challenges of life which is to ***remember*** who you are. You are a magnificent human ***Being.*** It is okay if you believe you are broken or that there is something wrong with you. It is a place to start. As you move through letting go of those beliefs then you will see, know, feel, and experience your completeness. Thinking you are broken or defective will be a thing of the past.

As you re-connect with the truth and power within you, noticing and using reflective mirrors to release attachments will become a natural part of your daily routine. You are growing and expanding your understanding and awareness of yourself, which requires wonder more than fear. Granted, at times you will feel fear and other lower vibrating feelings. They are not bad because they are lower vibrating, they are denser which makes it harder to move through them. They are also your teachers. Remember, feelings are *in-form-ation*. They are informing you of what needs your attention and focus.

Staying on the transformation pathway allows for more practice understanding yourself, embracing feelings, thoughts, and beliefs, as well as observing and using reflective mirrors. As discussed earlier, freedom from the bondage of self is a primary goal in life. This allows for addictions, attachments, and other self-destructive behaviors to melt away. When you are free of the heaviness there is more room to love, accept, and be your true self. As you embrace you, you will share that love you feel for yourself with your loved ones and the world, giving them permission to do the same. Taking 100% responsibility for yourself, your actions, thoughts, feelings, and beliefs provides the opportunity for pure bliss and freedom. Neville Goddard aligned with this idea of living. He said:

"How can a shadow be causative in your world? The moment you give another power of causation, you have transferred to him the power that rightfully belongs to you. Others are only shadows, bearing witness to the activities taking place in you. The world is a mirror, forever reflecting what you are doing within yourself. If you know this, you are set free."

Freedom lies within you. No one can give it to you or create it for you. You must seek it within yourself. As you become more familiar with centering, it becomes easier to take 100% responsibility for your life. Remember, it is a process. Centering within gives you the ability to use the outside world as a tool to understand yourself more thoroughly. There are levels of understanding that must be embraced before moving to the next one. Give yourself permission to grow and let go of any need to know everything. Have compassion for all parts of you. You did not know what you know now, a year ago. So judging that part of you is not helpful. Embrace curiosity and wonder as you notice your breath. Remember, your breath keeps you grounded and centered. ***Always, go back to the breath.***

Chapter Thirteen:

Trust the Process

A re you fully or partially committed to your change process? Think about it for a moment. Now assess where you are. Wherever you are is exactly where you need to be. Remember, you are building internal self-trust which takes consistency and persistence. The important fact is that you have begun the process. There is no going back at this point. Your awareness has increased whether you recognize it or not. If you are uncomfortable, good! That means your reality has been challenged and you are ready for what is to come.

Remember to honor, embrace, and release any resistance or fear that occurs as you move through your process. Remind yourself daily that there is no timetable for transformation. It occurs as it is supposed to within each of us. We all have things to process, explore, and release. You are not alone in your experience. There is love and support all around you whether you know it or not. The energy that created you never stops and never dies. It is the eternal flow of life that loves and supports you. Most of us have forgotten this truth and cycle in suffering. Yet, suffering is needed because it expands your consciousness and embraces your truth, power, and essence. This is the paradox. We need suffering to experience separateness, and we need to let go of suffering to return to oneness.

The questions, tools, and stories shared in this book are designed to open your mind and boost your sense of exploration and wonder. Use all the tools regularly. Contemplate your world, your awareness. Challenge yourself and shift your reality. Yes, life can be difficult, but it can also be magical and magnificent. The contrasts provide the rich experiences we have yearned for since birth. As you practice embracing them with love and acceptance, maintaining the flow of life will become second nature.

The beauty of this personal growth is that you can never fully return to the old you. You are new and

110

fresh. You are now on a new pathway of expansion. Yes, as discussed, there will be pain involved. Letting go of old behaviors tends to be difficult for most of us. But now, you have reached the end – the end of a journey, and are now embarking on a new one filled with contrast and curiosity.

Take a moment, breathe in and state this vow out loud: *I WILL NEVER EVER GIVE UP ON MYSELF!!* This is your commitment to you. You are important and special, and you deserve all the love in the world. The best person to give that to you is *YOU!* No one truly gives up on you. You give up on yourself. The mirror is reflected back to you by your loved ones and peers. If you feel or have felt that before then somewhere within yourself, you have given up on you. Assess where you are. Honor, embrace, and release what is surfacing and step back into your power. Take things one day at a time and even one moment at a time. Each moment, each tear, each breath is precious, no matter what your experiences have been.

One of the biggest lessons I have learned while walking the path of transformation has been to forgive myself quickly. I am not perfect. I have emotional meltdowns, I get angry, sad, and frustrated. Limiting thought patterns run through my mind at times. The key is to allow them to flow by. It works. I do it regularly and it leads me to self-forgiveness.

We tend to think there is something wrong with us if we have lower vibrating feelings which are typically considered negative or bad. Those feelings let you know what is going on within your body and mind. It is impossible for them to be bad. Society has labeled them incorrectly. It is time for change. All you must ask yourself is, "If I think my feelings are bad, does that support me loving myself?" The answer is no. If you believe your feelings are bad, you will repress and suppress them, which leads to self-destructive behaviors, making it more difficult to love yourself. Feel them and let them go. Your mind will likely tell you a self-defeating story about yourself and the feelings you are having. Allow the memories, the beliefs, to flow through you as best as you can. Elicit the breath to assist you as you release those things that are holding you back. Move back into your truth, acceptance, and beingness.

Take a moment now, pause, and notice your breath. Pay attention to how it feels as you take a breath in and allow it to flow out. Do you notice any sensations in your body? Are you tense, calm, numb, at ease, or in pain? Go back to your breath. What do you see around you? What shapes and colors do you see? Are they bright or dim? Take another breath. Focus on what you hear. Do you hear the wind, your breath, animal sounds? Another breath and release. What do you taste? Sour, sweet, bland? Allow your whole being to take in the world around and within you. This is being mindful and in the moment. Nothing is ever wrong in the moment, no matter where you are. This is the beauty of life. We get to choose how we perceive it.

As far as we know, the caterpillar does not have a conscious understanding that it is a caterpillar and that it will become a butterfly. It moves through life flawlessly. Meaning, it flows with the energy of life. When its internal guidance system says it is time to spool its cocoon, it finds a safe place and proceeds to move into its process of transformation. Within the chrysalis, it becomes completely unrecognizable. It loses its previous form and begins to take shape into its next level of magnificence.

This is the process for us all. We move through different forms throughout our lives. The difference is that the caterpillar knows it is one with all things and it trusts the flow of life. We have conscious thought which gives us an extra challenge. This is by design. It is not a punishment or a negative flaw. It has a higher purpose. You have been given everything you need within you. It is your job to recognize that and accept that it is true. It takes time and experience for most of us to embrace this truth. That is why I have given you tools to assist you as you find your truth and learn to love, accept, and be yourself. The Universe has provided both beautiful and appalling reflections for you to resist or accept. It is up to you to decide and see that everything around you **IS** a part of you.

Take a moment and think of something beautiful, something that brings warmth into your heart. It can be a person, place, or thing. Someone or something you admire. Allow the feelings to get stronger as you notice your breath. All that you see, feel, know, and are experiencing as you think of another person, situation, or thing, are in you. Embrace the feelings and sensations. All the love and admiration is magnificent, and ***SO. ARE. YOU.***

It has been an honor to share with you. May your life be filled with contrast and wonder. Peace, Love, & Laughter to you!

About the Author

Susie Armstrong is a gifted writer, healer, actor, and mother. She was born in Oklahoma City, Oklahoma and raised by a fun, talented, sassy mother, and a few interesting father figures. She loves connecting with loved ones, animals, nature, and other likeminded humans. Her passion is to continue to share love with the world through her writing, acting, and healing gifts. Susie is a Licensed Professional Counselor, a Licensed Drug and Alcohol Counselor, a Certified Professional Hypnotherapist, and a Certified EFT Practitioner. Susie is an expert in helping people implement change, by teaching them daily self-care tools to improve their ability to connect with themselves and others.

Printed in Great Britain
by Amazon